Akathist
to
Saint Basil of Poiana Marului

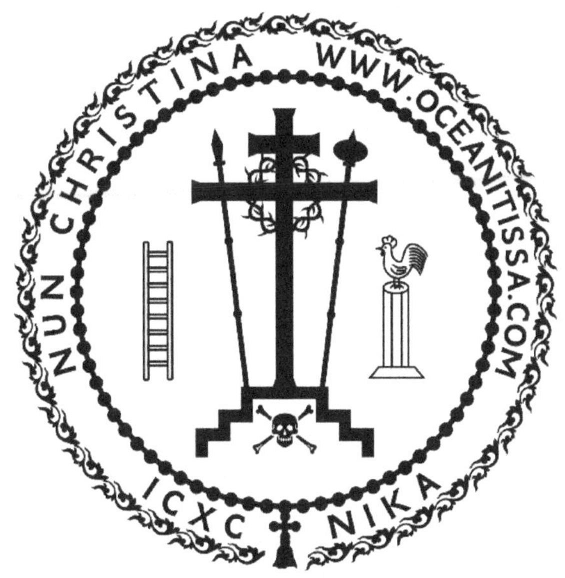

Anna Skoubourdis
Nun Christina

Published by: Virgin Mary of Australia and Oceania 2022 ©
oceanitissa@gmail.com
www.oceanitissa.com.au
Youtube: Nun Christina Oceanitissa

Subscribe to receive updates and Orthodox Christian creative media

www.oceanitissa.com

Troparion — Tone 8

Version 1

By a flood of tears you made the desert fertile, / and your longing for God brought forth fruits in abundance. / By the radiance of miracles you illumined the whole universe! / O our holy father Basil, pray to Christ our God to save our souls!

Version 2

Teacher of true reverence for God, adviser of monks, preacher of grace, teacher of the prayer of the pure mind, Reverend Father Basil, always ask Christ God to save our souls!

Akathist

Kontakion 1

To him who was a pure vessel of the Holy Spirit, the straightener of monks, the shining height of humility, the right balance of abstinence, and the strong intercessor of the prayer of the heart, Reverend Father Basil, let us offer prayers for our deliverance and sing to him: Rejoice, Pious Basil, great precant of Christ!

Ikos 1

From a young age, you showed yourself to be a lover of monastic life, Father Basil. You have boldly forsaken all worldly care and with love, you set out on the rough path of asceticism. Therefore, with humility and a voice of joy, we sing to you:
Rejoice, sweet-smelling flower planted in the garden of ascetic life;
Rejoice, the one who always talked to Christ through prayer;
Rejoice, for you have spent your monastic life in hardships;
Rejoice, for you resembled the angels through your ascetic life;
Rejoice, dweller with the saints who have pleased God;
Rejoice, for you have made the Buzău Mountains a Romanian Athos;
Rejoice, great lover and follower of the teachings of the Holy Fathers;
Rejoice, for you have fed yourself from the divine Scriptures;
Rejoice, for, through you, the name of Jesus was glorified;
Rejoice, for you have taught your disciples humble living;
Rejoice, the one who always prays to God for us;
Rejoice, Pious Basil, great precant of Christ!

Kontakion 2

Who will not bless you, Father Basil, the one who skillfully knew how to drive away the spirits of deception through a clean and pleasing life to God, for you have shone like a torch in the garden of the Mother of God - on Romanian soil - where you incessantly sang to God: Alleluia!

Ikos 2

You have been a shining beacon for the monks of the Romanian monasteries, Blessed Father. The example of your deeds and the fragrance of your teachings have led many to fulfill ascetic virtues and improve their lives. Therefore, receive these praises from us:
Rejoice, tree planted in the garden of the Romanian people;
Rejoice, for, through you, the land of our country has been blessed;
Rejoice, for we, the Romanians, have you always praying to God;
Rejoice, for you have become the guide of monastic order;
Rejoice, for you are among the lovers of faith;
Rejoice, for you have directed your steps towards Wallachia;
Rejoice, for in these lands you have proclaimed God;
Rejoice, for you strengthened the communities of our monasteries;
Rejoice, for you have guided many to the ascetic life;
Rejoice, you who lived on the plains of Buzău;
Rejoice, for you were an example of prayer for the monks at Poiana Mărului;
Rejoice, Pious Basil, great precant of Christ!

Kontakion 3

Lover of Jesus's prayer and living in the silence of the ascetic life, you showed yourself, Pious Father Basil, and, being in the flesh, God made you worthy to sweeten yourself from the fruits of the imperishable goodness of the Kingdom of Heaven and the sight of the happiness of heaven, singing with the angels continually: Alleluia!

Ikos 3

Called by God to the priesthood, Venerable Father Basil, you were afraid of this Holy Mystery; therefore, we humbly cry out to you:
Rejoice, for you were worthy of the grace of the priesthood;
Rejoice, for you have served together with the angels;
Rejoice, for you have given yourself to God through piety;
Rejoice, for you have shared divine teachings to many;
Rejoice, for you were worthy of great gifts from God;
Rejoice, the one who dedicated his life to serving Christ;
Rejoice, for you shine in spirituality;
Rejoice, for you are now serving in heaven with the saints;
Rejoice, you who honor the priesthood of Christ;
Rejoice, ornament of honor of pious monks;

Rejoice, for you were of great use to your disciples at Poiana Mărului;
Rejoice, Pious Basil, great precant of Christ!

Kontakion 4

Through you, Reverend Father, many monks and faithful discovered the practice of the Jesus prayer through which they were filled with divine grace, glorifying Christ unceasingly. That is why, with a voice of thanksgiving, we sing, together with all the saints, to God: Alleluia!

Ikos 4

Your life, indeed, has been a spiritual ladder to heaven, made wise by God; for you worked the barrenness of the desert with your tears, and with your prayers, you rose to the likeness of God as far as is possible for men; therefore, with joy, we bring you these praises:
Rejoice, zealous in the ceaseless calling of the name of Jesus;
Rejoice, for you have been enlightened by the spirit through prayer;
Rejoice, for you have united your soul with God;
Rejoice, for you have gained spiritual peace through piety;
Rejoice, for you have strengthened your body against temptations through fasting;
Rejoice, for we have learned the love of God since youth;
Rejoice, for you taught us to pray to the Lord mindfully;
Rejoice, for you have always prayed with the angels;
Rejoice, you who interweaved prayer with work;
Rejoice, that you taught the hermits to humble thought;
Rejoice, you who made Paisius Velichkovsky a monk at Athos;
Rejoice, Pious Basil, great precant of Christ!

Kontakion 5

With joy, Praised Father, all the groups of monks and the assembly of the faithful perform your honorable commemoration; for you have clothed yourself with good deeds as a valiant soldier of Christ, and with true love, you fenced your life pleasing to the angels, who sing with you to God: Alleluia!

Ikos 5

Let us praise today the earthly and God-pleasing angel, Reverend
Basil, in the Church of Christ, singing:
Rejoice, morning star shining like gold;
Rejoice, torch-bearer of the monks;
Rejoice, most fragrant shoot of the wilderness;
Rejoice, sweet-smelling rose of hermits;
Rejoice, guide of the wanderers;
Rejoice, sweet-smelling larder of ascetic hardships;
Rejoice, for you have conquered the pride of the flesh that covets
earthly things;
Rejoice, for you have desired the beauty of spiritual life;
Rejoice, for you have become worthy of speaking with Christ through
prayer;
Rejoice, for you have filled yourself with the Tabor light;
Rejoice, for the image of Christ has borne fruit through you;
Rejoice, Pious Basil, great precant of Christ!

Kontakion 6

Like the seer of God, Moses, you have entered the truly understanding
cloud of visions and have known that God reveals Himself to the one
who renounces himself and lets Christ live in his heart and soul, and
through the Holy Spirit, ceaselessly sings: Alleluia!

Ikos 6

Through you, Venerable Father Basil, the monastic life at Poiana
Mărului was established according to the order of Athos, where
fasting and prayer are the paths of perfection, on which, fulfilling
them with love, we rise to the height of heaven. Therefore, we too,
striving to follow them, honor you with these songs:
Rejoice, you have conquered the unseen enemied through humility;
Rejoice, lover of monastic hesychia;
Rejoice, skilled counselor of ascetic monks;
Rejoice, for you have established community life in monasteries;
Rejoice, for you guided the brothers from the monasteries to the
spiritual life;
Rejoice, for you have taught many monastic vows;

Rejoice, you who put good order in the monasteries under your
guidance;
Rejoice, you who had many disciples around you;
Rejoice, great lover of the prayer of the heart;
Rejoice, the honor of monks everywhere;
Rejoice, spiritual ornament of the Diocese of Buzău and Vrancea;
Rejoice, Pious Basil, great precant of Christ!

Kontakion 7

Knower and fulfiller of the Holy Scriptures you showed yourself,
wonderful Father Basil, these helping you to understand the works of
God from the nature of things and to strive in the hesychast life,
towards the union with Christ, incessantly singing: Allcluia!

Ikos 7

We marvel at your wisdom, Venerable Father Basil, which you
abundantly demonstrated in your understanding of the Holy
Scriptures, from which you learned humble contemplation in Christ.
For this, we reverently sing to you:
Rejoice, interpreter of the Holy Scriptures;
Rejoice, keeper of the Holy Tradition;
Rejoice, ever thinker of the word of God;
Rejoice, fulfiller of the evangelical commandments;
Rejoice, exhorter to living the divine teachings;
Rejoice, for you have become rich from the treasure of the Holy
Scriptures;
Rejoice, you who found strong support in the holy writings;
Rejoice, for you drank from the spiritual water of the Holy Fathers;
Rejoice, for you were enflamed by the powerful word of Christ;
Rejoice, for you have followed, according to the example of the
Reverend Fathers, the monastic life;
Rejoice, for you taught your disciples to live in brotherly love;
Rejoice, Pious Basil, great precant of Christ!

Kontakion 8

Separating yourself from worldly tumoil, you have fulfilled the hermit
life, resembling the fathers of the desert, beloved of God. For this,

together with them, we honor you, Reverend Basil, singing to God:
Alleluia!

Ikos 8

Most praised Father, we truly understood that the life of hermits is
blessed, seeing your peaceful ascetic life. For, arming yourself with
the divine longing, you changed the barrenness of the desert into a
field bearing spiritual fruit. This is why we sing to you:
Rejoice, you who, by restraining the body, resembled hermits;
Rejoice, that you became an example to the hermits;
Rejoice, for you put the devil to shame with fasting and prayer;
Rejoice, for you were a great herald of the Philokalia of the Fathers;
Rejoice, for you have been nourished by the teachings of Saint
Gregory of Sinai;
Rejoice, for you have tasted the sweetness of the prayer of Jesus from
Saint Isaac the Syrian;
Rejoice, for you learned sobriety in prayer from the Reverend John
Climacus;
Rejoice, for you followed the Holy Fathers in everything;
Rejoice, for from Poiana Mărului you rose to the heavenly things;
Rejoice, dweller with God's saints in heaven;
Rejoice, you who always pray for our salvation;
Rejoice, Pious Basil, great precant of Christ!

Kontakion 9

Reverend Father, you showed yourself to be a fulfiller and preacher of
Christian virtues, and the strength of your words beautified with
brilliant ornaments the faithful of the ancestral Church, who,
following your teachings, learned to sing to God, the One in Trinity
praised: Alleluia!

Ikos 9

Blessed Father Basil, you changed all the monastic communities that
you advised into spiritual oases of deep Christian living; therefore,
marveling, we cry out to you:
Rejoice, you who left us soul-building words;
Rejoice, for many were enlightened by your teachings;

Rejoice, you who devoted your whole life to prayer and the writing of Philokalia;
Rejoice, for you resembled a bee that loves the sweetness of the flowers when reading the holy books;
Rejoice, you who taught the faithful how to understand the mystery of holy prayer;
Rejoice, chosen founder of many monasteries with the holy ordinance;
Rejoice, for you commanded your disciples to follow the monastic rule with sanctity;
Rejoice, for you have guided them towards the perfection of the angelic image;
Rejoice, for because you made Poiana Mărului a school of pure prayer;
Rejoice, for you have guided the hermits of the Buzăului and Vrancea Mountains;
Rejoice, Father of the monks and advisor of the faithful;
Rejoice, Pious Basil, great precant of Christ!

Kontakion 10

Blessed Father, you lived on earth like an angel, and after your departure into the unperishable, being ordained by God in the heavens, you found the life with the angels. Therefore, rejoicing in the unspeakable glory, you unceasingly sing with the heavenly hosts to the Most Holy Trinity the song: Alleluia!

Ikos 10

Saint Paul, the great Apostle to the Gentiles, wrote in the divine Scriptures that the saints judge the world, and the psalmist, under the inspiration of the Holy Spirit, said that God is wonderful in His saints; therefore, we too, knowing that God has glorified you in heaven, as you have glorified Him on earth, kneeling before your icon, Pious Basil, say thus:
Rejoice, you who have prepared your eternal dwelling in heaven;
Rejoice, for your name is written in the book of life;
Rejoice, for you have found great grace in front of God;
Rejoice, for you have fulfilled the word of the Gospel in everything;
Rejoice, for you have taught us to ponder at heavenly things;

Rejoice, you who taught us the great value of obedience;
Rejoice, for, by your care, you ordained disciples in twelve
monasteries in Buzau and Vrancea;
Rejoice, for Poiana Marului has become a beloved place through
you;
Rejoice, for the number of Romanian saints you have increased;
Rejoice, you who always pray for the relief of our hardships,
Rejoice, you who intercede for the salvation of all;
Rejoice, Pious Basil, great precant of Christ!

Kontakion 11

Reverend Father Basil, your life was a ladder to heaven, which you
climbed, through virtues, to God, to Whom all the glory and worship
is due, and to Whom we ought to sing the angelic hymn: Alleluia!

Ikos 11

After the toil of ascetic life, being winged by the love of Christ, you
reached heaven, where you received the rewards of your labors,
Blessed Father. And, shining in the unspeakable light of God's glory,
do not cease to comfort your sons who struggle amid life's troubles,
crying out:
Rejoice, for your life was a continual holy sacrifice;
Rejoice, for you have prepared for yourself treasures in heaven with
your good deeds;
Rejoice, for you have moved with your soul to heaven, through death;
Rejoice, for you taught us to forsake worldly things;
Rejoice, for you have given us an example of humility through your
life;
Rejoice, you who led the monks to frequent confession and
communion;
Rejoice, for you have taught us to think of things above;
Rejoice, you who by testament left holy order in the monasteries;
Rejoice, for you protect us from temptations and troubles through
your holy prayers;
Rejoice, you who urged us to rise from the defilement of sins;
Rejoice, comforter of monks and faithful believers;
Rejoice, Pious Basil, great precant of Christ!

Kontakion 12

Reverend Father Basil, preacher of the prayer of the heart and teacher of self-restraint you have shown yourself; for your many labors, the world honors accordingly, giving glory to God, to Whom we also sing: Alleluia!

Ikos 12

You have proven yourself as a beacon of the true faith and an image of the meek, Reverend Father Basil, by which, amazed, with joy in our voices, we cry out to you:
Rejoice, you who dwell in heaven with all the saints;
Rejoice, you who have been fed the Bread of Life from infancy;
Rejoice, for, above all, you have chosen the angelic path of monasticism;
Rejoice, for you have thought of God day and night through prayer;
Rejoice, you who tasted the joy of heaven here on earth, through spiritual life;
Rejoice, you who instilled in us the spirit of Jesus' prayer;
Rejoice, for your prayers had ascended to heaven like sweet-smelling incense;
Rejoice, you who gathered the oil of joy in the candle of your soul;
Rejoice, you who taught everyone to ask for God's mercy;
Rejoice, for you have strengthened yourself spiritually by carrying the Cross of Christ;
Rejoice, spiritual guide of the famous abbot Paisius from Neamț;
Rejoice, Pious Basil, great precant of Christ!

Kontakion 13

O thrice-blessed, Pious Father Basil, the chosen ornament of monks, the holy joy of hermits, the steadfast pillar of patience, the silent trumpet of the prayer of the heart, angelic mind that multiplied the talent entrusted by Christ, hear us, the unworthy, who are engulfed by troubles and temptations, and pray to God to make us worthy, at the right time, of His heavenly Kingdom, so that we may ceaselessly, together with the angels, sing to the Most Holy Trinity: Alleluia!
(*Repeat this kontakion three times.*)

Repeat Ikos 1 and Kontakion 1.

Ikos 1

From a young age, you showed yourself to be a lover of monastic life, Father Basil. You have boldly forsaken all worldly care and with love, you set out on the rough path of asceticism. Therefore, with humility and a voice of joy, we sing to you:
Rejoice, sweet-smelling flower planted in the garden of ascetic life;
Rejoice, the one who always talked to Christ through prayer;
Rejoice, for you have spent your monastic life in hardships;
Rejoice, for you resembled the angels through your ascetic life;
Rejoice, dweller with the saints who have pleased God;
Rejoice, for you have made the Buzău Mountains a Romanian Athos;
Rejoice, great lover and follower of the teachings of the Holy Fathers;
Rejoice, for you have fed yourself from the divine Scriptures;
Rejoice, for, through you, the name of Jesus was glorified;
Rejoice, for you have taught your disciples humble living;
Rejoice, the one who always prays to God for us;
Rejoice, Pious Basil, great precant of Christ!

Kontakion 1

To him who was a pure vessel of the Holy Spirit, the straightener of monks, the shining height of humility, the right balance of abstinence, and the strong intercessor of the prayer of the heart, Reverend Father Basil, let us offer prayers for our deliverance and sing to him:
Rejoice, Pious Basil, great precant of Christ!

Prayer to Revered Father Basil of Poiana Marului

Holy Reverend Father Basil, chosen of God and heir of the Kingdom of Heaven, who live together with the angels and the saints, we pray to you with tears and humility: deliver us, through your holy prayers, from the multitude of temptations and troubles, from the hurtful lusts of the flesh and from the evil thoughts that come upon us. Be the intercessor of those in the monasteries who, out of love and faith towards the Lord Jesus Christ, have left all worldly cares to always serve God with you in the ascetic life. You are also an intercessor for those who honor the name of Jesus Christ and the one, holy,

ecclesiastical, and apostolic Church. Reverend Father, we address you
this humble prayer, which you may take before the heavenly Father
like some sweet-smelling incense. Make us have in mind and heart
the prayer of Jesus. Unite all Christians in the same righteous faith
and make us worthy to attain the happiness of heaven forever. Amen!

Dismissal prayer.

Biography

Saint Basil, the Elder of Saint Paisius Velichkovsky (November 15), was born toward the end of the seventeenth century. He received monastic tonsure at Dalhautsi-Focshani Skete in 1705 or 1706, laboring in asceticism with great fervor.

Saint Basil was ordained to the holy priesthood, and became igumen of Dalhautsi in 1715. He remained in that position for twenty years, and was a wise instructor of monks, teaching them obedience, humility, and the art of the Jesus Prayer.

The fame of this great spiritual Father began to spread, so that even Prince Constantine Mavrocordat heard of him. Saint Basil's community became known as a spiritual school of hesychasm, based on the wisdom of the Holy Fathers. When the number of his disciples increased until there was no longer room for all of them at Dalhautsi, they settled in other Sketes in the area. In this way, his influence and teaching spread to other places, inspiring a spiritual renewal of Romanian monastic life in the eighteenth century.

Saint Basil renovated the Poiana Marului (Apple Orchard) Skete near the city of Romni-Sarat between 1730-1733, then moved there with twelve disciples. In addition to his duties as Igumen of Poiana Marului, Saint Basil was the spiritual guide of all the Sketes in the Buzau Mountains. One of his most famous disciples was Saint Paisius Velichkovsky, whom he tonsured on Mount Athos in 1750.

The holy Elder Basil also wrote introductions to the writings of Saints Gregory of Sinai, Nilus of Sora, and others who wrote about the spiritual life, guarding the mind, and on the Jesus Prayer. He taught that the Holy Scriptures are a "saving medicine" for the soul, and recommended reading the Holy Fathers in order to obtain a correct understanding of Scripture, and to avoid being led astray through misunderstanding. Saint

Basil also warned against any inclination to excuse ourselves and our sins, for this hinders true repentance.

Saint Basil fell asleep in the Lord on April 25, 1767, leaving behind many disciples. His influence has been felt in other Orthodox countries beyond the borders of Romania.

Books published by Nun Christina Oceanitissa:

The collective works of St Nektarios of Aegina.
The Philokalia 5: The full text in English.
The collective works of Elder Cleopa.
The Anacreontic Poems by Saint Sophronius Patriarch of Jerusalem.
The Life of Saint Paul of Thebes the First Hermit.
The Devil: The Cause of Sin by Saint John of Kronstadt.
Faith and the Orthodox Church by Saint John of Kronstadt.
The Monastic Rule of Saint Pachomius the Great.
Supplicatory Canon and Akathist to St Paisios.
Supplicatory Canon and Akathist to St Porphyrios.
Supplicatory Canon and Akathist to St George.
Supplicatory Canon and Akathist to St Anastasia.
Supplicatory Canon and Akathist to St Anna.
Supplicatory Canon and Akathist to St John the Russian.
Supplicatory Canon and Akathist to St Ephraim of Nea Makri.
Supplicatory Canon and Akathist to St John Maximovitch.
Supplicatory Canon and Akathist to St Dimitri.
Supplicatory Canon and Akathist to St Joseph the Hesycast.
Supplicatory Canon and Akathist to St Luke the Surgeon.
Supplicatory Canon and Akathist to St John the Baptist.
The Way of a Pilgrim.
Conversation with a Grieving Man by St Dimitri of Rostov.
The Inner Man by St Dimitri of Rostov.
Orthodox Prayer Book.
Daily Orthodox Prayer book.